MW01463400

The Psychology of Abusive/Predatory Relationships

Alan

Thank you so much for your support & kindness!

[illegible] J Houston

The Psychology of Abusive/Predatory Relationships

~

How to Detach from and Avoid These Toxic Relationships

~

Miranda J. Houston

iUniverse, Inc.
Bloomington

The Psychology of Abusive/Predatory Relationships
How to Detach from and Avoid These Toxic Relationships

iUniverse books may be ordered through booksellers or by contacting:

iUniverse
1663 Liberty Drive
Bloomington, IN 47403
www.iuniverse.com
1-800-Authors (1-800-288-4677)

ISBN: 978-1-4759-3396-3 (sc)
ISBN: 978-1-4759-3397-0 (hc)
ISBN: 978-1-4759-3398-7 (e)

Library of Congress Control Number: 2012912177

Printed in the United States of America

iUniverse rev. date: 09/20/2012

Don't hate the predator, as it is the predator's nature to hunt prey, but do avoid relationships with these dangerous creatures.

I want to acknowledge that predators can be male or female; however, this book is designed for women who are in predatory relationships where the predator is a male. The dynamics of predatory relationships where the female is predator and the male is prey or in same-sex relationships are different, although the outcome is very much the same. Therefore, while this book has been designed for women, it can also be helpful to men and those in same-sex predatory relationships. Also, the focus of this book is on predatory relationships as opposed to abusive relationships. All predators are abusers but not all abusers are predators and the difference between these two types of relationships will be explained in the first chapter.

This book is dedicated to all women who have fallen prey to predators.

Self Help Book

This book is classified as a self-help book and has been designed for quick and easy reading. The information contained in this book is aimed at an audience that includes women and adolescent females. This information can also be of assistance to males and those in same sex relationships.

Predatory relationships can cause intense emotional pain, and many women avoid seeking help due to embarrassment or self-blame. Please note that you are not alone in this. Seeking help from a professional therapist is as healthy as going to see your doctor for chest pain, stomach pain, or any other health-related issue.

This information is neither intended nor implied to be a substitute for professional medical and/or psychological advice. It is a tool to increase your insight and awareness of predatory relationships, and it offers suggestions as to what you can do to detach from and avoid these toxic relationships. Information contained in this book should not be used as a substitute for professional advice; therefore, if you believe you are in a predatory relationship as defined in this book, as stated above, you should seek the guidance of a licensed professional counselor or therapist. If you or anyone you know is having thoughts of suicide or self-harm, please call 911 immediately and ask for help.

Acknowledgements:

I wish to acknowledge GOD who is the author of all creation. Without GOD, I'd be nothing.

I want to acknowledge my Father and Mother who taught me about GOD.

I want to acknowledge my siblings, my children, grandchildren, nieces, nephews, cousins and in-laws.

I want to acknowledge all of those who have played a role in my journey.

Contents

Introduction

To my beloved sisters who are hopelessly trapped in relationships where life has become nothing more than torture and all that surrounds them has become meaningless. To my beloved sisters who have somehow normalized the violent shocks aimed at quenching the beautiful and wild nature of a woman's soul. To those who have normalized that which is abnormal, even when it is depleting them of the energy that is necessary to survive and free themselves from the predator's rage. I say to you, "There are more than fifty ways to release your lover."

If you are reading this book, I applaud you for taking the first step toward detaching from and/or avoiding predatory relationships. This book will aid you on your journey toward setting yourself free and breaking the cycle of predatory relationships.

When your instincts have been damaged and you've come to know only pain that which is normal has no meaning and becomes an illusion— something out of reach and unreal. When you reach this state, you have successfully normalized the abnormal. The predator knows and understands your vulnerable spots and knows exactly how to tap into the deepest desires of your heart. In this way, he is able to create an illusion so distracting and irresistible that you signal to the predator that you are willing to become his victim. In essence, you unknowingly give him permission to victimize you. He is then able to gain access to your life, including your sexuality, your finances, and your energy, to which he is not entitled. He conveniently seduces you into surrendering to his whims using the power of the libido.

To return to a state of normalcy, you first need to understand how you arrived at your current state. You need to understand the nature and the psyche of a predator. You must repair your instincts and get to know and make friends with your vulnerabilities. You need to understand the power of your libido, gain control of it, and guard it. Finally, you will need to alter your state of consciousness, unlock and remove the chain from your heart and release your lover. It is time for a new start.

When you release your lover, focus on your needs, and take care of yourself, the universe will respond and support you. Once your libido is under lock and key and the chain is removed from your heart, the predator loses all power. That's when you gain sufficient energy to begin to heal your wounds and repair your instincts. Starting over means focusing on what you want out of life, devising a plan, and going for it using the energy of the predator's rage, which has now become *your* rage, to drive you. The confusion in your head begins to clear, and you gather incredible strength and intuition. You are now free to recreate your life.

I have had my own struggles as prey to the predator, and it is with sincere appreciation of my experience, however painful, that I write this book. My hope is to help women across all cultures gain valuable insight and life-changing energy so that they detach from and avoid predatory relationships. Finally, I write this book in hopes of helping women discover the gifts within themselves and call forth the pleasures of life that the Universe is waiting to release to them.

For many of you, this book will be your safe journey out of and away from predatory relationships. For others, it will be your guide to avoiding these painful relationships. For those of you who have adolescent daughters, this book will be instrumental in guiding them through these years so that they avoid predatory relationships.

CHAPTER ONE: THE PSYCHE OF A PREDATOR

All creatures must learn that there exist predators. Without this knowing, a woman will be unable to negotiate safely within her own forest without being devoured. To understand the predator is to become a mature animal that is not vulnerable out of naiveté, inexperience, or foolishness.

—Pinkola Estes, *Women Who Run with the Wolves*, 1992

You cannot protect yourself from predators of the human kind if you don't know that they exist or who they are. Therefore, this chapter is dedicated to helping you understand who these predators are and how they function.

One important distinction to be made before moving on is the difference between a predator and an abuser. There is currently a lot of research in the area of domestic abuse, but little attention has been given to the issue of predatory relationships. The distinction between an abuser and predator can be found in the paragraphs to follow. As stated earlier, all predators are abusers, but not all abusers are predators.

The *United Nations Population Fund (UNFPA),The State Of World Population: Ending Violence Against Women And Girls 2000 report* found that "many cultures condone or at least tolerate a certain amount of violence against women." (UNFPA, The State Of World Population: Ending Violence Against Women And Girls 2000 pg. 26)

In some cultures, according to, The State Of World Population: Ending Violence Against Women And Girls 2000, men hold the belief that they have the right to beat their wives. Behaviors such as, " not obeying the husband, talking back, refusing sex, not having food ready on time, failing to care for the children or home, questioning the man about money or girlfriends or going somewhere without his permission" (The State Of World Population: Ending Violence Against Women And Girls, 2000 pg. 26) gave a man the right to beat his wife. Even in this great country of ours, men at one time in history took it as their right to beat their wives, and this was viewed as a family matter. People turned their heads; some women suffered in silence, while others normalized this behavior. Some women held the belief that if their spouses did not beat them, they did not love them; others took a beating as a matter of foreplay before sex.

It is not uncommon for young men who have witnessed their fathers beat their mothers to internalize this behavior as normal. As a result, they too beat their wives. Some men may have impulse control or anger issues, and although they know it is wrong to beat their wives, they may lose control and hit anyway. Some of these men may feel genuinely remorseful about what they've done.

In summary, an abuser may very well have a conscious and most likely has been influenced by what was once a societal norm. They may very well understand what they are doing is wrong, but due to conditioning early on in life or societal influences, they may struggle with how to change their behaviors. They may also have anger issues or problems with impulse control. These men may benefit from some type of therapeutic intervention.

A predator is someone without a conscience and whose sole intention is to exploit another human being for his own benefit. He has no attachment to the woman he holds captive as prey and sees her as "food for the kill." Predators roam the cities looking for vulnerable women, just as animals in the wild search for food. They are wired very differently from the average human being and do not have the capacity for genuine warmth, caring, and compassion for others. While predators are usually charming initially, they also can be physically abusive and use physical abuse as a means of control.

In summary, predators do not have a conscience and lack the capacity to genuinely love another human being. They see others as a means to an end or "food for the kill." They are wired very differently and most likely will not benefit from therapeutic interventions. They are likely to use the tools they gain in therapy as a weapon in future relationships.

According to Robert Hare in his book *Without Conscience*, there are as many as 2 million psychopaths (predators of the human kind) lurking among us in North America. He also estimates that there are as many psychopaths as there are schizophrenics (Hare, 1999 pg. 2).

Take heed, though, of this warning: *predators are not out to have a relationship.* They are out to take from you what they can. This includes your energy, your finances, your sexuality, and anything else of value that the predator deems necessary for his survival. Predators prey on those who they perceive as vulnerable, naïve, or weak. They study their environments and seem to have the natural ability to zone in on those with weakened defenses, such as the naïve and vulnerable female. They will pursue relentlessly until the prey capitulates. In the eyes of the predator this capitulation is viewed as an agreement by the prey to become his victim. The prey on the other hand believes she is entering into a genuine relationship.

In many instances, the predator preys on women who are the kind and nurturing type or they may be single, lonely or widowed. Predators feel that they are entitled to your resources as payment for services rendered. That service being some unmet need they perceive you as having.

One must come to an understanding of predators of the human kind in order to successfully navigate their environment without being snared. I will define them in four ways: psychological, religious/spiritual, folklore/fairy tales, and the animal kingdom. Some people may not be able to identify with the psychological definition of a predator, but the other definitions may resonate with some, moving their spirits and thereby facilitating learning. Again, you must come to know the psyche of a predator before you can protect yourself from one. The following is a smorgasbord of information, and you may choose the definition that speaks directly to you about the psyche of a predator.

Psychological

Sigmund Freud, one of the earlier pioneers in the field of psychology, describes three stages of personality development: the id, ego, and superego. Below I offer a simple description of these terms.

At the id stage of development, the individual wants what he wants when he wants it with no regard for whom he steps on to get what he wants. An individual at this stage has not yet developed a conscience. At the ego stage of development, one learns a sense of right and wrong, cooperative living, and respect for others and makes decisions that are based on these principles. Finally, at the superego stage of development, one begins to respond to a higher calling. This person's values are in alignment with their spiritual and moral development. At this stage, one makes decisions based on what is ethically and morally correct.

That being said, I define a predator as a person without a conscience, who functions at the id level with a grossly underdeveloped ego, and who is totally void of a super ego. This also describes what used to be defined in the *Diagnostic and Statistical Manual of Mental Health Disorders* as psychopathic personality disorder but is now defined as antisocial personality disorder. While it sounds a bit "spooky," the term *psychopathic personality disorder* is more likely to catch one's attention, whereas *antisocial personality disorder* could easily be misinterpreted by those outside of the field of psychology as someone who is introverted, timid, or shy. Therefore, for practical purposes, a predator as described in this book can also be described as a "psychopath."

It should be noted that the term *psychopath* has also been associated with serial killers, rapists, and sexual predators or pedophiles; however, not all psychopaths engage in these heinous crimes. In fact, many of them value their freedom and operate under the radar of the law to avoid imprisonment. They could be your boss or coworker, your next-door neighbor, your significant other, your daughter's boyfriend, or your son's girlfriend.

So while all predators are not violent killers, etc., they are toxic beings and can cause as much destruction in a woman's life as a tornado ripping through your neighborhood. They can wreak enough havoc in a woman's life that they leave her feeling traumatized, spiritually broken, and emotionally empty. Many women who have reached this state experience such intense emotional pain that they have considered suicide as their only way out. Unfortunately, some women succeed.

Predators will move on to the next victim without any remorse or guilt for the havoc that they have wrought. Predators lack the capacity to see others as human beings and value others no more than they value a bug or spider. For example, in his book *Without Conscience*, Hare illustrates how a predator might think: "Do I feel bad if I have hurt someone? Yeah, sometimes but mostly it's like uh … (laughs) … how did you feel the last time you squashed a bug?" (Hare, 1999 pg. 33)

During a television interview on the popular news show *48 Hours*, defense expert Dr. Thomas Sachy explains "the science of insanity." He points out that the psychopath has a serious defect in the area of the brain that controls empathy, warmth, caring, and compassion. He further reports that if you view a brain scan of a normal individual who has been exposed to a situation that elicits one of the above emotional responses, you will see a lot of activity in the area of the brain that controls those feelings. However, if you view the brain of a predator (psychopath) under the same conditions, you will see little or no activity. In other words, predators are wired differently and lack the capacity to care for others. They are cold, aloof, and unable to empathize with other human beings. This is why it's easy for a psychopath to destroy another human being physically and/or emotionally.

Religious/Spiritual

Lucifer, also known as Satan, is described in biblical terms as a fallen angel who thought of himself as equal to Yahweh (God). He set out to overthrow Yahweh and was driven out of the heavens and stripped of his power. Lucifer is also described as the prince of the air and author of all evil. He roams the earth seeking power and destroying others to get it. His primary purpose is to kill, steal, and destroy.

Lucifer is a trickster and is skilled at misleading those who are vulnerable. He can mask himself as someone who can love and be trusted and thereby entices his prey to follow a path that will ultimately lead to their destruction. He strips them of their resources, which they need for their survival, and they are then left as dry bones. Lucifer, on the other hand, has gained a source of power and strength. He then quickly moves on to his next victim.

In Christianity and many other religions, people aspire to develop their personalities at the superego level. As stated earlier, Lucifer (as in the psychological definition of a predator) functions at the id level, has a grossly underdeveloped ego, and is totally void of a superego. Lucifer has no conscience and is usually depicted as a devil with a pitchfork.

Folklore/Fairy Tales

Fairy Tales and folklore are myths and tales that have been passed from one generation to the next for the purpose of teaching and learning. One such fairy tale is that of the failed magician. The failed magician is the apprentice of a wizard. In an attempt to become superior to the wizard, the apprentice (failed magician) ventures beyond his capacity. In the process, he fails and is thrown from the club, losing all of his gains. As an outcast, the failed magician has no energy and is unable to generate light which is necessary for his survival. His only salvation is to try and destroy others and steal their energy so he can create light.

Bluebeard is an example of a failed magician. In the Bluebeard story, Bluebeard was an outcast who had no energy or light. He was also a wealthy aristocrat and serial killer who was shunned and feared because he had a rough look and an ugly blue beard. Because of his status as a wealthy man, Bluebeard was able to take on multiple wives for the purpose of stealing their energy so he could generate light. Mysteriously, all of his wives disappeared. (The story of Bluebeard will be discussed in detail in chapter 4.)

The Animal Kingdom

Predators in the animal kingdom are the carnivores that rely upon meat to survive. They prey on other weak and vulnerable animals. This is how they have been designed; it is in their DNA. When predators in the animal kingdom go after prey, they see the prey as nothing more than "food for the kill," and they are not wired to have empathy for those they pursue as prey.

A lion will zone in on a herd of elephants or water buffalos and will seek out the most weak or vulnerable. This is usually a baby or one who is weakened by age or sickness. When the chase is on, the lion focuses on what it wants relentlessly and usually will not give up until he has successfully captured his prey. The prey will usually give in and signal to the predator that he is willing to become victim when it realizes its capture is inevitable.

It is what it is, and whether you see the predator as a psychopath, Lucifer, failed magician, or lion, in each form, he has the same goal—to drain you of your energy, resources, and anything else that he deems necessary for his survival.

There are several warning signs that may indicate you are dealing with a predator. The predominant feature of a predator is the lack of a conscience. If you are in a relationship with someone who can commit horrendous acts against others (things that would make a normal person feel remorseful or ashamed) with no remorse, shame, or guilt and who can inflict pain onto others as if they were nothing more than objects, you should see a therapist without delay, as you may very well be dealing with a predator. Below I have listed other features of a predator and some of the behaviors you may experience in a predatory relationship.

Take note also that the features listed below may exist in a non-predator as well; however, if you notice too many of these traits and the person does not appear to have a conscience, you should seek professional help immediately.

Isolation: In the animal kingdom when a predator hunts prey, it spots the most weak and vulnerable one of the herd and then sets out to separate it from the rest of the herd. This makes it easier for the predator to capture and hold on to its prey. A predator of the human kind will employ the same tactic, setting out to isolate and destroy important relationships so that your only source of information comes from him. This makes it easier for him to brainwash a woman and therefore control her mentally and emotionally.

Superficial charm: A predator has the ability to charm another just as a cat charms a bird right into its paws. He will stare at you as if you are the apple of his eye, making it difficult to resist his seduction. He may be good at making you laugh and telling convincing stories that capture your imagination. He knows exactly what you want to hear and will convince you that he can give you the world, even though he has no resources of his own.

Grandiose sense of self: A predator has to make himself believe that he is a powerful and important person in order to convince others of the same. He feels entitled to others' resources and will convince you that he is entitled. A predator has grand schemes as to how he will become rich and famous. Even though he lacks the motivation or skills to follow through, he will convince you to invest anyway, leaving you with no return on your investment.

Lack of remorse or guilt: A predator has no conscience; therefore, he doesn't feel any guilt or remorse for his behavior. Regardless of how much pain he may cause others, he will walk away without feeling a thing. When a lions hunts and kills a baby elephant, does it feel guilty? The same is true of a predator of the human kind.

Deceptive: A predator will lie and at the same time tell the truth, making it difficult to see through his acts of deception. He will tell you what you want to hear, sometimes even telling you the truth about his motives in a subtle, joking manner. When you confront him, he will tell you that he told you the truth, which he did. If you bought into what you wanted to hear, he will blame you and accuse you of not listening to him or taking him as a joke.

Manipulates others for self-interest: A predator is quite manipulative and can pull a trick out of his sleeve as quickly as a magician. He may go out of the front door while making you feel guilty over something he did and come in through the back door demanding an apology in the form of cash or some other valuable resource.

Lacks empathy or compassion: A predator's brain is wired differently; he doesn't have the capacity to show compassion or have empathy for others. He is only concerned about getting his needs met, and you just happen to be the catch of the day, month, or year. He cannot see you as a human being with feelings; instead, he sees you as "food for the kill."

Dull emotions: A predators has no real emotions. Even his laughter can be shallow. He doesn't know when it is appropriate to laugh or cry and may even be caught laughing at someone's pain and suffering. If someone is crying, a predator finds himself at a loss as to what to do and may feel that the emotional person is mentally weak.

Impulsive behavior: A predator, although calculating when it comes to something he wants, can also be very impulsive, even to his own detriment. He doesn't always know how to look out for his own best interest due to impulsivity. He acts on impulse, because he is looking for immediate self-gratification—never mind if it's at someone else's expense, and never mind the havoc he created. He just felt like doing something.

Need for frequent stimulation/excitement: A predator can't stand regimen. While some predators may hold a job, most are likely unable to get up and go to a job on a daily basis. A predator likes the thrill of being able to manipulate someone into taking care of his needs. He is constantly on the prowl, studying his targets and inventing strategies for "getting over" and keeping his victims in line. He can't stand orderliness, as that would be too boring, and he may be prone to filth and degradation.

Takes no responsibility for own actions: A predator is not capable of taking responsibility for what goes wrong in his life. If for some reason his next victim refuses to roll over, then something must be wrong with that person for refusing to be a victim. A predator doesn't see anything wrong with victimizing others; therefore, he doesn't need to change anything about his behavior. If something goes wrong in the predator's life, it is because something is wrong with his victim. A predator will even punish the victim because something has gone wrong in his life.

Sexually provocative and inappropriate: A predator has no boundaries when it comes to sex. Sex is a bargaining tool, and he will perform sex acts with anyone for his own pleasure, for money, or for anything else that furthers his cause. He will frequently use sex talk as a means of enticing unsuspecting victims and use the power of the libido as a means of control over others.

Inability to commit in a relationship: A predator has no sense of commitment. He may have multiple partners and rotate his victims in and out of his life based on his current needs. He may have been married multiple times only to leave spouses with no explanation, simply because he had no more to gain in the relationship. It is now time to move on to the next victim.

Parasitic lifestyles: A predator is not a provider and usually has nothing to offer in a relationship. He is able to quickly attach himself to unsuspecting, vulnerable women who are caring and compassionate and who can provide for him. A predator is likely to drain his victim mentally, emotionally, and financially and move on when he is either fully gorged or there is nothing left.

CHAPTER TWO: THE NAÏVE WOMAN AND THE VULNERABLE SPOTS IN A WOMAN'S PSYCHE

As we have evolved as human beings, creating culture and tradition and moved on to modern civilization we have also tampered with the soul of a woman. We have dampened her spirit and annulled her sexuality. We have deadened her senses, drowned her creativity and stolen her instincts. We have fed her fairy tales and rendered her helpless. In the final analysis of it all we have made her prey to the predator.

—Miranda J. Houston

A naïve woman can be defined as one whose instincts are not intact. She is neither aware nor in tune with her vulnerabilities. Naïve women most likely don't have knowledge that predators of the human kind exist, have been improperly socialized through culture and religion to view life in an unrealistic or idealized fashion, and may have experienced some form of abuse or trauma that has dulled or damaged their instincts. They have been robbed of their natural ability to recognize danger. They are open to the power of suggestion and very easily influenced and manipulated by others, thereby making them easy prey.

Unfortunately, females are reared to be vulnerable from the start. They are taught to play with dolls and feminine toys, while boys are taught to play with cars and trucks. Boys are taught that it is okay to be aggressive and to defend themselves, while girls are conditioned to be passive and submissive and to rely upon men to protect them. Girls are dressed in cute little dresses, taught to be dainty, and conditioned to pay special attention to their appearance so that they look "attractive." They are taught to be tenderhearted and to take care of others. They are taught to put the needs of others before their own needs. They are further taught by religious leaders to love unconditionally and to be forgiving. Finally, they have been conditioned to fall in love, marry, have children, and live happily ever after.

What has gone wrong is that society has failed to warn women that predators of the human kind exist and failed to prepare women to avoid them. Women who have become involved and married to predators are encouraged by religious leaders and others who don't recognize that predators of the human kind exist to stay in these marriages and pray for the predators' souls to be saved. A woman may be told to turn the other cheek and "kill him with kindness." When he leaves, the woman is encouraged to pray for his return.

Predators love to prey on the population of women who uphold these religious principles, because they know that they can hold onto their prey for as long as they need to and can exit and return as often as they like. This population may feel guilty for talking back to and confronting predators, because they are led to believe that they are to be submissive to their husbands. Under normal circumstances, the above conditions would be blissful for women who aspire to live by these religious principles and who are with men who have a conscience and fear God.

We have failed to warn women that they must take care of themselves before they can successfully care for others, just as a breast-feeding mother cannot produce milk for her child without feeding herself first. When we fail to care for ourselves and instead place our complete faith and trust in another human being to care for us, we render ourselves vulnerable to others. This is risky business, as human beings are not perfect and therefore prone to error. To put your faith and trust in a predator, however, would be the same as offering oneself as a sacrifice or "food for the kill."

Some women have been traumatized at some point in their lives, and without some type of therapeutic intervention, these women may find themselves vulnerable to predators. For instance, a woman who has been sexually abused may carry a belief throughout life that she has no power to say no to others, or she may normalize this abuse and carry the belief that somehow her body is for the pleasure of others. Some women who have been physically or emotionally abused may normalize abuse and carry the belief that a relationship is not fulfilling in the absence of some form of abuse.

Women who are vulnerable do not have defenses that are working properly. In a normal situation, a woman will only let her defenses down after she has thoroughly assessed and found a pattern of consistent positive messages and behaviors that suggest it is safe to do so. Women who are vulnerable have few or no defenses working for them and may trust easily and give men access due to their inability to detect and resist that pattern of inconsistencies.

Two of the most vulnerable spots in a woman's psyche that give a predator complete access include her heart and her libido. These are the areas that a predator focuses on to gain power and control over women as prey.

Libido

Predators are sexually provocative and can be very seductive and sensuous. These factors may be great relationship enhancers in a normal relationship; however, for the predator these are just tools to be used to gain control of a woman. A predator frequently uses sexually provocative language to cause sexual arousal but very often will not deliver unless there is something for him to gain. A predator is not so much interested in the act of sex as much as he is interested in the secondary gains.

In this way, sex is nothing more than a bargaining tool. He further creates the illusion of the fantasy relationship that he believes women dream about with the ultimate in the sexual experience. He will deliver this ultimate sexual experience at intervals that are similar to intermittent reinforcement, which can cause a powerful form of addiction. Therefore, if a predator can gain control of your libido, he will be able to control you. Because of this, it's important to guard your libido.

The Heart

Predators also know our deepest desires of the heart, such as to be loved unconditionally, to be cherished, to be the apple of someone's eye, to be special, to have heavy romance, and to have hot and steamy sex. A predator can deliver on these things 10 percent of the time—just long enough to capture the heart. He may send flowers, wine and dine you occasionally, and pay special attention to you and your needs until he figures out what it takes to captivate your heart. Once he captivates your heart and gains your loyalty, he quickly changes the name of the game, and you find yourself giving in to his whims to keep the relationship going. Occasionally, he will deliver some token of appreciation, such as flowers or other gifts, to deceive you into thinking that he really cares for you. In reality, it is really a form of reinforcement to keep the relationship going. Because of this, it's also important to guard your heart.

Take note that being vulnerable in a relationship can be a rewarding experience mentally, emotionally, and sexually if the relationship is healthy. A healthy relationship can mean many things, so for ease and simplicity, I define a healthy relationship as one where your partner is kind, loving, and trustworthy and looks out for your best interest. At the end of this book, I have included a reference list that contains additional resources you can refer to for more information on healthy relationships. If you have trouble understanding the dynamics of a healthy relationship, you should see a therapist who specializes in relationship issues for assistance.

Lastly, being vulnerable does not make one weak; rather, it is a sign of one's ability to engage in life and to connect at a deeper level to other human beings. It is an act of courage; however, you do have the right to decide who you will be vulnerable with and who you will "dance" with.

CHAPTER THREE: THE DANCE BETWEEN PREDATOR AND PREY

Among animals there is said to be a mysterious psychic dance between predator and prey. It is said, if the prey gives a certain kind of servile eye contact, and a certain kind of shiver that causes a faint rippling of the skin over its muscles, that the prey acknowledges its weakness to the predator and agrees to become the predator's victim.

—Pinkola Estes, *Women Who Run With the Wolves*, 1992

Predators target women from across all cultures, socioeconomic statuses, and races. In many cases, these are very high-functioning women who have access to money and other resources that a predator needs for his survival. A predator may also have multiple relationships and rotate women in and out of his life based on his needs at the time. Basically, a predator is looking for women who are willing to dance with him, and anyone with a vulnerability that she is not in tune with can become a target.

Predators have the natural ability to spot a vulnerable woman and the skills to lure her to him. In many cases, there is not necessarily a physical attraction to the predator other than the illusion or fantasy that gets created in a woman's mind once she allows a predator to get in her space. Some women, who have been in predatory relationships where there was unfinished business, may unconsciously attract other predators to continue the dance.

Consider the statement "opposites attract." Predators go after women with traits that are the complete opposite of their own traits. Predators attract to themselves women who are kind, compassionate, loyal, and tenderhearted. These women are usually very spiritual and have the capacity to love unconditionally. Even more important to a predator than the above traits is a woman who is also naïve and vulnerable.

Because they possess the above traits, these women can sometimes believe that they are indispensable and that "love" will conquer all. They also tend to hold the belief that they can conquer and tame the "bad boys." Even when their relationships begin to go south, these women don't give up because they love unconditionally. Predators are able to attract women like this and are able to touch these women in untapped places due to their weakened defenses.

A predator is often viewed as exotic and exciting because of his charm, wit, and ability to move a vulnerable woman's spirit with a kind of certainty (however false) that comes once in a lifetime. Because of this, a predator is able to seduce a vulnerable woman into believing that the relationship between them is sacred, special, and like no other relationship she has ever experienced.

Due to the skills of the predator, the unsuspecting, vulnerable, and naïve female is easily attracted to and captivated by the predator who is able to connect with her almost instantly. The unsuspecting female misinterprets this as a sign that he is really into her, and she may enjoy the intensity of the pursuit. She is drawn in by the romantic and sexual fantasies that the predator is able to articulate so well, and these fantasies enable him to keep her mesmerized—that is, stuck on her emotions, which deadens her ability to respond to her instincts.

A predator utilizes a number of deceptive devices or emotional manipulation techniques to keep you dancing with him. He may tell you what you want to hear, but in a subtle or joking way he may also clue you in to who he really is. When the relationship starts to deteriorate, he is then able to place the responsibility onto you. He told you who he was, and as far as he is concerned, you were not listening or you thought he was joking. You assumed that he was on board with your needs and wants, although his behavior clearly said otherwise, and he assumed that you were on board with his plan because you were with him.

Because the predator is able to capture your heart and your libido, he also is able to control you using the power of suggestion. He then eats away at your self-confidence and self-esteem. The predator will make suggestions, which one will quickly acquiesce to as a way of pleasing him even when these suggestions go against one's own standards. He will give you mixed messages to keep you off balance and keep you guessing as to what his likes and dislikes are. This creates a huge distraction that makes it difficult for you to discern or question what his real motives are.

A predator will blame you for everything that he is and everything you are not and will cause you to begin to question and doubt yourself. If he is cheating, he accuses you of cheating. If you speak to another man he will go into a jealous rage and accuse you of being a cheater. He is a natural liar, and will constantly accuse you of being a liar to distract you from the fact that he is the liar. If you say you are going to the store but change your mind or you forget to tell him you stopped at a friend's house, you become a liar and deceiver.

The predator will emotionally blackmail you using other women to keep you in check. If he wants something from you and you refuse, he will threaten to get it from another woman. He knows you will give in because you can't stand the thought of him being with another woman.

At this point, the predator has you reacting to fear and your actions are now based on the mind chatter that he has created which causes you to doubt and question yourself. This mind chatter is directly related to the actions of the predator, which have been designed to keep you blinded so that you are not able to see the light at the end of the tunnel and therefore unable to escape his mental grip. There is constant mind chatter with yourself regarding whether he loves you or not and whether he is cheating. You actually know the answer to these questions, but fear prevents you from the acceptance of this reality.

This is the point when you begin to believe that you are to blame for what is going wrong, and you struggle in pain to fix whatever you believe is the problem. As you struggle, the predator is able to take more from you, because you now feel responsible for the relationship. He will guilt you into doing things, such as giving up your finances, valuable possessions, or anything else that is necessary for his survival. He will share with you plans for your future, convincing you to invest, and you give in out of fear and unwarranted guilt.

At some point in this relationship, you lose the ability to focus and take care of yourself and lose perspective on other important aspects of your life, including your job, children, extended family, and friends. From time to time, the predator will give you a token of appreciation for being his victim and to keep you loyal to him. This token may come in the form of sex, flowers, or a night out on your money.

Soon, the pain of leaving is greater than the pain of staying; at this point, you have successfully normalized the abnormal. Somehow you believe that he will deliver on his promises to you and make things right. It is this unfinished business that keeps you holding on. Your only salvation is that at some point, when he has nothing else to gain or finds someone with more to give, he will decide to leave you.

Consider the following: "He will choose you, disarm you with his words and control you with his presence. He will delight you with his wit and his plans. He will show you a good time, but you will always get the bill. He will smile and deceive you, and he will scare you with his eyes. And when he is through with you, and he will be through with you, he will desert you and take with him your innocence and your pride. You will be left much sadder and for a long time you will wonder what happened and what you did wrong. And if another of his kind comes knocking at your door, will you open it?" (Hare, 1999 pg. 21)

CHAPTER FOUR:
DISARMING THE PREDATOR

***Predators know no boundaries;
therefore you must draw the line.***

—Miranda J. Houston

To disarm the predator, one must detach. When you detach, you create the necessary space to disarm and move away from the predator. Up to this point the predator has been able to seize and hold you captive using a series of emotional manipulation techniques described in the previous chapter on the dance between predator and prey. The two most powerful techniques involve capturing your heart and controlling your libido, and you will need emotional distance in order to disarm the predator.

Detaching emotionally from a romantic partner can be traumatic and painful. To conquer this pain and to detach from the relationship successfully, one must make friends with the pain. While the thought of making friends with pain may sound impossible, it is absolutely attainable and necessary for your growth. When you embrace pain, it becomes less hurtful and easier to deal with. In the song Good Morning Heartache, which was recorded by Billie Holliday in 1946, she sings, "Might as well get used to you hanging around, good morning heartache sit down." This is an example of acknowledging and embracing the pain. Suppressing the pain, running from it, and trying to be tough will not get rid of the pain; instead, it will prolong it. Facing the pain, however, will be a powerful aid in your recovery from it.

On the other hand, you don't want the pain to consume you, which could drive you into a state of despair. You can starve the pain to keep it from consuming you. In his book, *The Power of Now*, Eckhart Tolle, describes a process he calls "dissolving the pain body" (Tolle, 1999 pg. 29). In this process, he describes how one can acknowledge his or her thoughts and feelings to cut off and starve the pain. Based on this process described by Tolle, I believe that thoughts and feelings feed off of each other and keep each other going. If it happens to be a cycle of negative thoughts and feelings, they will keep the pain alive; this is how one becomes consumed by their pain, which leads to despair.

To break this cycle, one must prevent the thoughts and feelings from connecting. By doing so, you break the cycle of pain. You can break this cycle by acknowledging your thoughts and feelings as they come up. Simply acknowledge your thoughts by saying to yourself, "I hear you." To acknowledge your feelings, you can say to yourself, "I feel you." While acknowledging these thoughts and feelings, you also want to focus on what is going on around you at that moment. This is called being in the present moment. The past has come and gone, and you can't do anything about that. We don't know the future, because it has not come yet. All you have is right here and now.

When you acknowledge your thoughts or feelings and pay attention to the here and now, the thoughts and feelings will cease. By acknowledging the thoughts and feelings as they surface, you also prevent them from connecting. When they connect, they feed off of one another. As a result, a vicious cycle develops, causing you to be in a constant state of emotional pain, which, as noted earlier, leads one to despair. These negative thoughts and feelings will attempt to come back, but if you practice this technique on a regular basis, it will allow you to continue with life until you have successfully worked through the pain of this relationship.

There will be times when you will need to allow the pain to surface, preferably when you are in the comfort of your own space. Having a crying session is a healthy and necessary component of detaching from this romantic attachment. Crying is actually part of the grieving process and can aid in expediting your healing.

Detaching from the predator may also require you to alter your state of consciousness and release the predator at a soul level. This letting-go process, or release exercise, is a healthy way of letting go of your romantic attachment to the predator. It aids you in completing the unfinished business that keeps you stuck and can deter you from getting into another predatory relationship. This is important because a predator will not work toward closure and will most always leave unfinished business.

The unfinished business has to do with the many promises he has made. It is common for the woman to get stuck on this unfinished business and wait for him to make good on his promises or "make things right." The predator knows that as long as there is unfinished business he can return. There are women who allow predators to return over and over, hoping that he will make things right only to be heartbroken again. Women who do this focus on the 10 percent of good from their predators without realizing that they are not capable of fully and completely being that 10 percent.

To detach and release a person requires you to go inside of yourself and emotionally release the person. Doing so will further create the emotional distance you will need in order to heal from your romantic attachment. The emotional manipulation used by the predator may leave you feeling as though you are on a roller coaster. It is difficult to get off of a roller coaster as long as it is moving. In other terms, you can become so emotionally enmeshed with this person that you can't think, see, or feel your way out. When you release this person from within, you will create the space needed to stop the roller coaster and get off, thereby prying yourself away from this person emotionally.

The following release exercise has been inspired in part by Kathryn Alice and her work on *Releasing a Person* (Alice, 2006) or detaching from a romantic attachment. To do the release exercise, you will need to be in a quiet place. You can darken a room and light candles if you like. Make sure you have tissues nearby, as this exercise can generate tears. You can also play soft instrumental music; you don't want to play music with lyrics at this time, as you will not be able to focus on the release exercise. DO NOT ATTEMPT TO DO THIS EXERCISE WHILE DRIVING!

Start by relaxing yourself. Take time to breath in and out slowly, and as you do so, allow the muscles in your face and neck to relax. Continue to breathe in and out until you have relaxed the muscles in your shoulders, arms, back, legs, and feet. Spend some time just breathing in an out until you feel completely relaxed.

As you begin the release process, start by thinking of a time when you felt happy or loved. This could be your first camping trip, your first pet or a special moment between you and your parents or siblings or some other special person in your life. You want to get yourself in a place where you felt truly happy, loved and at peace. Pay attention to your body as it relaxes even more. Stay in this place for a moment.

As you feel ready, think of the person you want to release and try to see his face. For a brief moment think of any good times you may have had with this person. You don't want to focus on this for long because this is what has kept you stuck up to this point. You want to recognize and acknowledge that these good times were all a part of the ploy to exploit you. At this time you also want to acknowledge to yourself that there are more good times to come with someone who is right for you.

After a minute or so, think about the bad times in your relationship and the pain it has caused you. As you think back to the painful reality, see the person's face and recognize him for who he really is as opposed to the person you believed him to be. You can also say any last words that you would want to say to him, whether it is a simple good-bye or things you have been either unable or too afraid to say in the past.

The final step in the release process is to actually release him. At this point you, want to state his full name and then simply say, "I release you to the Universe. Peace and blessings to you and to me. Good-bye!" As you say good-bye, you also want to seal off access to your heart and libido by saying, "My heart and libido, as well as other areas of my life are now closed to you." You want to say these things aloud as you are speaking to your subconscious mind, and you want to give your subconscious mind a firm and sharp message.

You now want to take a moment to allow any sadness to surface. This is your time to grieve the relationship. Know that it is okay to cry, as it is all part of the grieving process and will aid in your healing from this relationship.

As you move on, please note that you may be tempted to get back into this relationship. Because of this, it's possible you may need to repeat the release exercise. You can also fight the temptation to reattach by staying in the present. You may find yourself looking back at the relationship in terms of what you wanted it to be or fearing that he will become the person you wanted him to be with someone else. Focusing on the past and trying to see into the future are the triggers that can lead to falling back into this toxic relationship.

You may also want to revisit the first chapter of this book ("The Psyche of a Predator") to ease your mind and assure yourself that the decision to end this relationship was an important and necessary decision. Understand that you were not in a healthy relationship and that your partner is unable to be what you want him to be. Due to the predatory nature of his personality, he does not have the capacity for a genuine, loving relationship. He is a predator; it's important to remember that a predator is looking for a source to meet his needs, not a relationship.

Lastly, you may want to take assertiveness training. Remember that predators pick up on body language. To be sure that you scare off all predators, it may be helpful to learn to talk and walk with confidence. A predator gains confidence when he knows you are insecure and afraid; he will spot and go after the most vulnerable. Many of prey are chosen simply because they look and act vulnerable.

I once went into a store after working all night. I was very tired and ready for bed. I walked as though I were struggling; to a predator, I would have looked vulnerable. While waiting in line, I realized a man was fixating on me for some reason. It dawned on me that I looked pretty beat up from working all night. He stared at me nonstop, so I changed my stance so as to scare him off. I got out of line and went into the bathroom where I splashed water on my face and changed my composure. I left the bathroom with a brisk walk and a look that would kill. Once back in line, the man stopped staring, because my composure had changed. I no longer appeared vulnerable. Predators don't want trouble, which is why they go after those perceived to be weak and vulnerable.

The next chapters will help you to avoid these toxic relationships in the future using the "power of instincts." You will also learn that this is not the end for you. You will be provided with valuable information to assist you in changing your relationship blueprint so that you can attract the kind of mate you desire. You will also affirm yourself and re-create your life. The Universe is waiting to open up a lifetime of possibilities for you.

CHAPTER FIVE: THE POWER OF A WOMAN'S INSTINCTS

A woman's instinct is her innate ability to see the unseen and to feel what can't be felt. It is her ability to hear the unheard and to smell what can't be smelled. It is her ability to taste what can't be tasted and to calculate what can't be calculated. It is her ability to act upon that which can't be acted upon and to see lines one and two and the line in between which can't be seen. It is her ability to tell the story which can't be told and finally, it is God's voice inside a woman's head guiding her journey through earth.

—Miranda J. Houston

Sir W. Hamilton defines instincts as "an agent that performs a work of intelligence and knowledge blindly and ignorantly" (Hamilton, 1913 n.p.). That being said, aside from the socialization process, some of the things we do are simply designed by nature.

Some activities associated with instincts are aimed at survival, including our need to fulfill hunger and thirst, to protect ourselves from danger, and to love and be loved. Our instincts can be viewed as our best friend. Although skeptics have tried for many years to categorize instincts as a secondhand emotion, scientists have been busy studying instincts and through lab experiments and brain scans have successfully proven that this trait does, in fact, exist. I describe instincts as our natural human intelligence and pose the question, why would humans be created without this survival instinct that even animals possess?

Martha Beck, PhD and graduate of Harvard University, discusses intuition in her book *Finding Your Own North Star.* In her book, she describes the "internal compass," (Beck, 2001 pg. xv) which I interpret as one's natural human intelligence or instinctive drive. She also shares multiple stories with the reader on those who have found their way by relying upon this natural intelligence. In an article titled "Wise Beyond Our Years," Bahram Akradi, who is the founder and CEO of Lifetime Fitness, cleverly describes instincts as "the intelligence of raw survival fused with the more miraculous and mysterious drives of the human soul" (Akradi, 2010 pg. 87).

In reality, who needs a scientist to confirm what we know through our natural human intelligence? It is through this gift that we naturally breastfed our babies and protected them from danger. It is through this gift that babies are able to find their way to their mothers' breasts and will cry and become fussy when they are hungry are wet. All over the universe there is a natural order.

In his book *The Seven Spiritual Laws of Success*, Deepak Chopra describes this natural order when he suggest, "Grass doesn't try to grow, it just grows. Fish don't try to swim, they just swim. Flowers don't try to bloom, they just bloom. Birds don't try to fly, they fly. This is their intrinsic nature" (Chopra, 1994 pg. 53). As we have progressed as a modern society, we have in many ways cut ourselves off from our natural intelligence and now rely upon textbooks to teach us something as natural as how to breastfeed a baby.

Our ancestors, who had no exposure to the modern amenities we are afforded today, relied upon their instincts for guidance on how to navigate and get their needs met in every area of life, from nourishment to mating to surviving in the wild. As we grow and develop, we intuitively gather information about our environment guided by our instincts. When danger is lurking nearby, we instinctively take flight. As we further grow, we are able to scan our environment and sniff out any dangers. We learn to calculate and navigate. We learn that there is a time to respond and a time to be still. Finally, all of the complexities of the instincts become perfected, and this intuitive knowledge is captivated to advance our cause and to aid in our own survival. This intuitive information gets passed on to our offspring.

All of this growth can be thwarted if a woman is improperly socialized or has experienced some form of abuse or trauma. These issues can cause a woman's instincts to be *dull* or *damaged*, rendering her vulnerable. The following are examples of *dull* or *damaged* instincts and stories to help you further understand the difference between the two.

Dull or Damaged Instincts

If a woman has *dull* instincts, her system of checks and balances is functioning at low capacity. On the other hand, if a woman has *damaged* instincts, her system of checks and balances is completely shut down.

You know your instincts are *damaged* when a predator crawls through the window and "even though they're wearing a ski mask, have a knife between their teeth, and a sack of money slung over their shoulder, we believe them when they tell us they're in the banking business" (Pinkola Estes, 1992 pg. 48).

The following is the folktale, a story about a tender woman who is unable to protect herself because her instincts are *damaged*:

The Tender Woman

The tender woman finds a half-frozen snake in the woods. The snake beckons her to pick him up and take him in so that he does not freeze to death. She believes him when he promises her that he will not bite even though he is a snake. She looks at him and notices that his pretty skin had been frosted with dew, and she decides without hesitation to take him in and take care of him. She wraps the snake up in a piece of silk and lays him by her fireplace with honey and milk.

Later, the woman finds that the snake has been revived. She picks him up and admires his beauty and feels good that she took him, because he would have died otherwise. She strokes him, kisses him, and holds him close to her. Instead of thanking her, the snake viciously bites her.

The woman cries out, "How could you? After all, I saved your life. You know that your bite is poisonous, and now I am going to surely die."

The snake replies with a silly grin, "You knew I was a snake before you took me in."

Your instincts are *dull* when you intuitively know the predator is a bank robber, and you allow his charm to override your intuition. Instead of the predator being a bank robber, he is now just a cute and eccentric banker.

The following is the story of Bluebeard and a young, naïve female whose instincts were *dulled*:

The Bluebeard Story

Bluebeard was a wealthy and lonely man with a rough look and an ugly blue beard. He had married many wives who all mysteriously disappeared. Everyone in the community was suspicious of Bluebeard, including the three beautiful daughters of a neighbor whom he had laid eyes upon as candidates for a future wife.

Bluebeard approached the mother of the three daughters and asked if he could marry one of them. The mother left it to the daughters to decide if they wanted to marry him. All three were weary of Bluebeard because of his ugly beard and his reputation of marrying many wives only to have all of them disappear.

He convinced the young women to visit his castle, and they reluctantly agreed. They brought friends with them, and Bluebeard showed them a good time. The younger daughter was beginning to see him differently and started to believe that he wasn't so bad after all and even convinced herself that his beard was pretty. She allowed his charm and riches to override her instincts, while the older daughters remained skeptical and unimpressed.

Bluebeard was able to charm the younger daughter into marrying him, and she went to live with him in his castle. One day Bluebeard announced to his new wife that he was going on a mission and would be leaving her home alone. He told her to invite friends over and enjoy his castle while he was away. He gave her the keys to every room in the castle; however, there was one room that she was forbidden to enter, and there would be dire consequences if she did. She agreed not to enter this particular room, although Bluebeard knew she would not comply.

After Bluebeard left, she invited over her friends. They went from room to room, admiring their findings. While her friends were visiting, the young woman got the sudden urge to enter the forbidden room, so she vanished for a moment to the far corner of the lower level of the castle and opened the door. There she found blood stains and the beheaded bodies of Bluebeard's missing wives. She began to tremble and dropped the key on the floor. When she picked it up, it was stained with blood. She tried to wipe it off, but the blood would not disappear and had penetrated the key, staining the other side.

When Bluebeard returned, she pretended that she had left the key to the forbidden room in her room somewhere. He continued to ask for the key, and when she finally gave it to him, he noticed the blood. Bluebeard immediately knew that she had entered the forbidden room. He told her that because she entered the room, she would take her place among the women she had seen.

The young woman cried at Bluebeard's feet and pleaded for him not to kill her, but he was heartless and had no conscience and insisted that she would die. She asked for a moment to tidy herself before her death, and he granted her this wish. In the meantime, the young woman summoned for her brothers to come and rescue her. Her brothers heard her cry and rushed to the castle to kill Bluebeard and rescue their sister.

In the story of the tender woman, the woman's instincts were *damaged* and totally shut down. She believed the snake when it said it would not bite and without hesitation she picked up the snake, even though by nature snakes will bite. In the story of Bluebeard, the young woman's instincts were *dulled*. She had some awareness of danger; however, she allowed Bluebeard's charm to override her instincts. She gave in to his whims and married him.

We must regain what was lost and stolen from us. We must go down beneath the surface to heal our wounds and rediscover the natural talents that were given to us by the Creator. We must view our instincts as our friend, as they are there to protect us. We must call up the blueprint of our past, explore where and how our instincts became damaged, and discover how we came to be captive, who our captors were, and why our instincts had not protected us.

For the moment, you must dismiss the part of the socialization process that instructs you, as a woman, to be nice, to smile, and to treat the enemy with kindness. In the process of being kind to a predator, a vulnerable woman subjects herself to the whims of the predator and becomes food for the kill. You must also dismiss the fantasies in your head about life and accept the realities that are covered up by these fantasies. Opening your eyes to these truths will ultimately set you free.

You will be set free, because with open eyes, you can now choose a mate who is void of predatory traits. With open eyes, you will be able to sniff out any discrepancies or inconsistencies in a person's behavior and move on just as the two oldest of the three young women in the Bluebeard story. It is the youngest, more naïve sister who succumbed to the happily ever after fairy tale and allowed herself to become the prey of a psychopath and serial killer.

You must get to know your real self as opposed to the person you have come to be as a result of socialization. In the story of the tender woman and Bluebeard, your real self would have sniffed out and discerned the dangers and would have gone in another direction. In the animal kingdom, it is natural for prey to run away from the predator. Even a developing lion cub will instinctively run away from what is perceived to be a threat.

When animals are threatened, the fight-or-flight instinct prepares them to either take flight, freeze, or fight. If it becomes necessary to fight, it is natural for an animal to show its razor-sharp teeth or tongue; in some cases, this is all that is necessary. In other instances, it is necessary to strike. Women have the same fight-or-flight instincts except in those cases where their instincts have been dulled or damaged.

A predator does not stand a chance with a woman whose instincts are intact or with another predator of the human kind, because he will be devoured. Furthermore, a predator has no interest in someone who is as cold and callous as he is. He is also not interested in someone who isn't going to give in under any circumstances and who will fight before becoming his victim. Predators are looking for the least amount of resistance; therefore, women whose instincts are not in tact are their primary targets.

Again, you have the skills necessary to navigate through life, but until you tap into your natural intelligence—that is, the instincts that have been given to you from the beginning by the Creator to protect and preserve yourself—it will be easy for you to fall victim to predators. The realities that you are living by are manmade and speak to ideal relationships. These realities are not necessarily bad, but for some, the ability to discern danger as it relates to relationships is absent.

To understand our instincts, let's examine a mother lion. When she senses that there is danger nearby, her flight-or-fight instincts automatically turn on, and she quickly takes her cubs and moves them away from the danger. If this lion is raised in captivity, she will never have the chance to grow and develop in the wild and sharpen her instincts. Her instincts will become *dull* or *damaged*, and if placed back in the wild, she might make mistakes that could be fatal to her and her cubs.

And so it is with women. When you have been traumatized or socialized in a way that actually shelters you and prevents you from learning to use your instincts to survive, you may make mistakes that can threaten your survival when placed out into the wild. In some cases, these mistakes can be fatal.

Steps to Take to Repair Damaged or Dulled Instincts

The process of repairing *damaged* or *dulled* instincts requires a woman to explore her past. If you were a victim of abuse as a child, it may be necessary for you to explore this with a trained therapist. If you associate love with any type of abuse, you may also need to do this work with a therapist.

You may need to explore relationships within your family of origin to determine if there was a pattern of abuse within your family. Ask yourself the question, who harmed me emotionally? Examine every relationship in your past where you felt hurt. This includes relationships within your family of origin, your teachers, your peers, and all previous romantic relationships. Write a story describing these relationships and how they may have impacted your life.

For instance, in my family of origin, I was a middle child and felt very insignificant. My parents were quite often so busy with my older siblings or younger sibling that I got lost in the shuffle. I wandered around in my neighborhood, and I felt l had to accept attention wherever I could get it. Sometimes that meant I had to fight for it or act out to get it. I remember as a kindergartener standing up before being called upon to answer the question; what comes after the rain? I was scolded and told to sit down because I thought that after it stopped raining the sun came out and dried it up. That is what happened in the song "Itsy Bitsy Spider," which we sang on a daily basis. The teacher frowned at me and if looks could kill, I would not be writing this book. The answer was that after the rain, came the rainbow. I was six years old and had seen plenty of sun after it had rained but had yet to see a rainbow. I felt conflicted and insignificant and betrayed by the song "Itsy Bitsy Spider." because in this song, after the rain comes the sun.

At some point I began to act out to get attention and was abused by the nuns who, at that time, felt entitled to abuse kids. By the time I reached fourth grade I was being abused physically, emotionally and sexually by my peers and adults including the nuns and priests. I had been trained to be a martyr saint by the Catholic Church and to turn the other cheek when someone was abusing me. I was told by my abusers not to speak up or harm could come to my family. I was socialized to wear dainty little dresses and to be a nice little girl. Overall, because I felt conflicted and insignificant and because of the abuse I experienced at the hands of people held in high esteem, I normalized these early life experiences. I accepted abuse as a norm, I accepted that I was insignificant, and I kept my lips tight. I also came to believe that somehow my body was meant for the pleasure of others.

As a teenager and an adult, I have encountered multiple predators along my journey, and because my instincts were damaged, I fell prey time and time again. The majority of my relationships were conflicted, and I felt insignificant. I came to believe that the relationship was for the man, and my happiness depended upon being his slave. I had no voice of my own. If a man were to tell me that the sky was blue, I agreed, but if in the same breath he said it was green, I would have agreed to that too. I was told that I was a victim, and as long as I believed that, I took no responsibility for my safety or happiness. I suffered in silence and always believed that harm could come to me or my family if I spoke out.

At some point in my life, I encountered a predator unlike any I had ever encountered before. It was at this point that the course of my life changed. It was either sink or swim, and I had to rely upon one of my most positive early life experiences for strength. I had a swim teacher who once told me to either sink or swim when I was on my last lap while trying to pass from intermediate swimmer to swimmer. I only had half the length of the pool left to finish, but I gave up to tiredness. I stopped swimming and started drowning. I was waiting for the instructor to stick the pole in the water and pull me out, but instead she told me to sink or swim. When I realized she meant it, I turned over and continued on my journey. I passed the test.

With the last predator whom I encountered, I found myself at a point where my spirit was nearly broken to pieces. It was at this point that I took responsibility for myself and decided that I was no longer a victim. It was at this point that I decided to gather my broken pieces and swim. I did my work, and when predators see me, they now run in the opposite direction.

After you have finished documenting your story, record how you felt while writing. For instance, when I started writing my story, I felt tense and my breathing started to get shallow. I was near tears and felt betrayed by that "Itsy Bitsy Spider" song. I was so hurt by that incident because I loved that song. I remember feeling crushed when the nun told me I was wrong and then frowned at me, as though I had done something terribly wrong. I started to feel pain in my chest as I thought about the betrayal of the priests and the nuns in the Catholic Church. I thought about the nasty little boys in my neighborhood and the dirty old men, and I started to feel fear. I thought about the predators in my life, and it was clear to me how I had become such an easy target. As I got to the end of my story where I began to take responsibility for myself and as I remembered passing that swim test, I started to feel a sense of power and triumph. I felt good, my body relaxed, and I could feel myself breathing a sigh of relief that this would never happen to me again. I am not a victim, but I am a strong survivor.

We usually attract or are attracted to what we are most familiar with, as you can see from my story above. If you have accepted a pattern of abuse, you may be unconsciously attracting abusive/predatory partners. Examine all of your romantic relationships and make a list of the positives and negative in each of them. Rate whether negative or positive behaviors were present in the relationship the majority of the time. For instance, were the negative behaviors present most all the time and the positive behaviors only occasionally?

In a predatory relationship, the predator can present himself as the person you want him to be 10 percent of the time, but this is not who he really is. You can say that who you met was really his public relations representative, but the person he is 90 percent of the time is who he really is. Again, we tend to attract what is most familiar. You will need to change your relationship blueprint to attract the kind of person you really desire. There will be more on this later, so save your list of negatives and positives for a later time in this journey.

Repairing damaged instincts also requires one to quiet the mind and listen to the body. Our minds are constantly chattering; however, most of this chatter can be discarded. Mind chatter is usually associated with things in the external, or things outside of ourselves. We frequently focus on this mind chatter to come up with solutions to complex issues. Getting in tune with your instincts will require you to focus on the internal and make decisions from the inside out (instincts given to you by the Creator) rather than outside in (what you learned from the socialization process).

If you are in a predatory relationship, chances are high that you have been relying upon decisions made from the outside in as a way to keep your romantic attachment to the predator going. You can't rely on the same framework of thinking that got you into the relationship to get you out of it. Quieting your mind and learning to listen to your body will enable you to be in tune with the internal and make choices from the inside out rather than outside in.

Your body does not lie and does not like being lied to. In order to access your natural intelligence, you must find quiet time on a daily basis to get rid of the mind chatter. An example of mind chatter could be obsessively thinking, "he loves me, he loves me not." The resulting conversation that runs through your head is fueled by the predator who is able to convince you that he loves you 10 percent of the time. The other 90 percent is doubt fueled by the inconsistencies in the predator's words and actions. This causes confusion regarding his love for you. Again, your body does not lie and does not like being lied to. The following exercise will help you to listen to your body and draw conclusions based on inside-out rather than outside-in thinking.

Think about a time when you felt loved and cherished or think about a time when you felt happy. Think back to how you smiled and imagine yourself being engulfed by love and/or happiness. Take note of your breathing patterns, the decrease in your muscle tension, and your pleasant facial expression. Your body expands, relaxes, and signals that you are in a loving and comfortable place.

Now think about a time when you felt hurt, betrayed, and unloved. Remember the pain, anger, and resentment you felt during that time. Take note that your body contracts, you start to get tense, and your breathing becomes shallow. Your body is signaling that you are in a bad place.

When you are in a good place, your body relaxes and the energy flow is smooth. Your body wants to continue to move in this direction and will give you signals indicating this. When you are in a bad place, on the other hand, your body will contract and restrict energy flow, causing you to become tense. When you keep moving toward what is not good for you, the body signals that this is not a good choice and will react violently when you ignore the signal. Think of it as something jumping up and down in your body saying, "No, please don't go there!"

Another way to get in tune with your instincts is to study the animal kingdom. Watch as predatory animals move in on their prey. The prey stops and listens as it senses danger. The prey then runs in the opposite direction, away from the perceived danger. A lion cub will run away from perceived danger and signal to its mother that it is in danger. We have the same sensory capabilities; however, we are not trained to use these capabilities. We sometimes go to the danger rather than away from it.

Imagine being approached by someone who is interested in pursuing a relationship with you. Your instincts, which have access to trillions of pieces of information, are instantly able to gather information about this person. If your instincts are not working properly, mind chatter will get in the way of you making the right choice. As you converse with this person, pay attention to your body and the signals that you pick up. If you feel your body contracting and tensing up and sense butterflies in your stomach, go in the other direction. Your body is telling you this is not a good place. If you feel good one moment but start to pick up a pattern of inconsistencies as you continue the conversation, your body will start to contract, signaling you to pay attention. Remember that a predator can say what you want to hear or show you what you want to see about 10 percent of the time. However, he cannot maintain it, which means you need to be aware that the first 10 percent of the conversation might be fun but won't last. Your body will signal when it is time to cut the conversation short.

Another way of getting in touch with your instincts is to pay attention to what your body is saying about your companion or perspective partner. How he makes you feel will tell you how he feels. If your companion makes you feel bad by belittling you with disparaging remarks about who you are, your sexuality, or your family, take note that this is how he feels. It has nothing to do with you. A predator can't radiate good feelings, because he doesn't have any to give. Under these circumstances, your body will begin to feel tired and drained. You may also have butterflies and other body sensations signaling to you that you are in a bad place and you need to protect yourself. In other words, it may be time to take flight.

Practice paying attention to people's actions compared to what they say as another way of sharpening your instincts. A predator can be a smooth talker and use kind and sweet words, but if his words aren't backed up by some action, your body will signal to you that there is a discrepancy between his words and deeds. Your body will send you a message of confliction. If your companion is saying that he loves and respects you and at the same time is emotionally blackmailing or bullying you, your body will pick up on this even though you may be experiencing mind chatter that is trying to defend and justify this conflict.

You can also use deductive reasoning to train your mind to pick up on inconsistencies in patterns of communication and behaviors in predatory relationships. An argument based on deductive reasoning examines validity and helps one to draw conclusions that are sound and rational. Below are examples of deductive reasoning:

My companion says he loves me.
Love is showing respect.
My companion does not respect me.
Therefore, in this scenario, your companion does not love you because love means respect.

My companion says he cherishes me.
Valuing and appreciating who I am is to cherish me.
My companion does not value or appreciate me.
Therefore, in this scenario, your companion does not cherish you because valuing and appreciating who you are is to cherish you.

My companion claims to be kind and considerate.
Being kind and considerate is to be sensitive to my feelings.
My companion makes mean and disparaging remarks about me.

Therefore, in this case scenario, your companion is neither kind nor considerate because being kind and considerate is to be sensitive to your feelings.

On a daily basis, practice putting together case scenarios using deductive reasoning and pay attention to any discrepancies you pick up on. You can also practice this exercise with friends and relatives. Let them know that you are working on developing your "shit detectors" so that you can weed out predators before they get too close.

Take note that you may find inconsistencies even in well-intended individuals, but remember that you are looking at patterns. You may occasionally pick up on an inconsistency but that doesn't put a person in a predatory category. If you however, are picking up a pattern of inconsistencies in your companion's words and actions, your body will sound off an alarm to let you know that something is not right. A predator can only hold it together and appear genuine for a short time, so it is up to you to tune in to his words and actions and pay attention to what your body is saying.

Learn to make choices that are good for you. I learned a great lesson on making choices from reading Deepak Chopra's book *The Seven Spiritual Laws of Success.* Here is my version of making choices based in part on the work of Deepak Chopra. In predatory relationships, the predator is there to exploit you for your resources and will take advantage of the fact that you care for him to get what he wants from you. Learn how to make choices that will not hurt you. For instance, if a choice you are about to make will help someone else but hurt you; it is not a choice you want to make unless you feel like sacrificing. Even so, these kinds of choices should be the exception and not the rule and should only be made when you feel a divine calling to do so.

In a predatory relationship, the choices one makes are usually to the benefit of the predator and to the detriment of the prey. Therefore, it is very important to understand what impact your choices will have on you as prey. For instance, if a demand is placed upon you for money and you need the money for your own survival, the answer is an automatic no because giving in to this demand will hurt you.

If a choice you are about to make will help you but hurt someone else, it is also not a choice you want to make. If the choice you are about to make is going to help both parties, then you may have a legitimate reason to make this choice. In this scenario, no one is hurt. Most importantly, learn to listen to your body's responses when making choices.

Another way to get in tune with your instincts is to explore—get to know and make friends with your vulnerabilities. This will trigger your instinctive drive to survive, as your instinct is your friend and is there to protect you. For instance, if you know you are vulnerable in certain situations, your body will instinctively lead you away from such circumstances. If you have recently detached from a predatory relationship, you are likely still vulnerable to this person. Coming in contact with him may trigger the attachment, and you may find yourself reattaching and starting the cycle all over. Acknowledging this vulnerability will give you the incentive to avoid any and all unnecessary contact with this person. It also allows you to keep your defenses up and resist his attempts to seduce you.

CHAPTER SIX: CHANGING ONE'S RELATIONSHIP BLUEPRINT

Without uncertainty and the unknown, life is just the stale repetition of outworn memories. You become the victim of the past, and your tormentor today is yourself left over from yesterday.

—Chopra, *The Seven Spiritual Laws of Success*, 1994

Things are in a constant state of change; in fact, change is the only thing that is constant. Therefore, we actually live in uncertainty without acknowledging it. Failure to acknowledge this reality and face it compels one to stay where they are. Sometimes it is difficult to move on from a bad relationship due to fear of uncertainty. Staying in a predatory relationship is destructive to your health and well-being, and that is a certainty. Changing your relationship blueprint is one way of avoiding predatory relationships in the future. To change your blueprint, you must learn to be comfortable with uncertainty.

A relationship blueprint is a pattern of mate selection based on earlier life experiences. We usually replicate what we are most familiar with and therefore attract or are attracted to those who fit within our frame of reference, which is based on these early life experiences. Changing your relationship blueprint will require you to move beyond this reference point. One must leave her comfort zone and drift into the realm of uncertainty. You will need to become comfortable with this uncertainty as you work on changing your relationship blueprint. Just as you get used to a new neighborhood, new city, new school, or new job, in due time you will get used to new experiences in relationships.

If you grew up in a family where the males were dominant and females were more submissive, you may tend to gravitate toward a mate who is a dominant male because that is your orientation. Similarly, if you were raised in a family where the male figure was abusive, you may gravitate toward a mate who is abusive. Your blueprint from this point forward may be set for abusive or predatory relationships.

Sometimes women who grow up in families where things appear fairly normal still have dull or damaged instincts due to the socialization process or trauma; these women may also find themselves in abusive/predatory relationships. In a case such as this, the woman's blueprint could very well become set for abusive/predatory relationships. We have all heard of women who have escaped abusive/predatory relationships only to find themselves in other bad relationships down the road. This is because their blueprints have been set for bad relationships. Some women also have unfinished business from previous relationships that leads them to attract other predators. This is a result of not allowing themselves to heal on the inside from their previous predatory relationships. This compounds the problem, and without some type of intervention, the pattern most likely will continue.

Changing one's relationship blueprint is a very important task for moving on, as you don't want to carry the past with you. It is one way of ensuring that you don't attract another predator of the human kind. Take note that this process will not happen overnight and will require some practice on your part. This is a time when you may also want to seek the help of a therapist to make sure that you are setting a healthy relationship blueprint. Below are two exercises to help you change your pattern of mate selection.

Exercise One

- Analyze those relationships formed early on in life, such as parents, siblings, teachers, etc.

- Compare those relationships to your current and previous relationships, including friendships and romantic attachments, and write down any similarities.

- Write a story detailing your history. Include family of origin issues if applicable and any relevance they have to your pattern of mate selection.

For instance, when I was a child, I was exposed to physical, sexual, and emotional abuse in the Catholic schools by both the priests and nuns who were held in high esteem. Some of the nuns were very dominant and controlling and demanded compliance with their rigidity, and several of the priests were friendly, charming, and sexually abusive. My father was very dominant and controlling, and my mother was very submissive, sweet, and nice. I became a target in my neighborhood for all of the dirty old men and nasty little boys and somehow came to believe that my body was for the pleasure of others.

It felt perfectly normal to me when I had my first real date with a pimp. Initially, I gave in to his seductions on the promise of marriage, but he was unsuccessful in his future endeavor to turn me into a prostitute. I believe that the values instilled in me by my parents and, ironically, the Catholic Church saved me. His seductions, considering my earlier experiences, felt perfectly normal until he tried to get me to engage in sexual activity with someone else while he got paid. The pimp did not get very far, but I was devastated. My next boyfriend was also dominant, abusive, and exploitive. Once again, I was very docile, sweet, and nice even though I was being abused and exploited. By this time, this pattern of mate selection was a norm for me, and every boyfriend I encountered after my first relationship was a predator of the human kind until I changed my relationship blueprint.

- If you are currently in a predatory relationship, on a separate piece of paper, write out a list of the predator's characteristics, both positive (those traits that gave you joy) and negative (those traits that caused you pain).

- Go back and visualize previous relationships that have been abusive/predatory and repeat the exercise above.

- Perform a ritual where you release all of the negative traits of your current and previous relationships. Take your list and shred it, burn it, or release it into a campfire, the muddy Mississippi, or a nearby pond. Whatever you choose to do, make it a ritual and formal good-bye to these old patterns. While doing so, say to yourself out loud, "I release these traits from my psyche, and I refuse to accept these traits in future relationships. I am entitled to joy in my life, and I call forth the pleasures of life that the Universe is waiting to release to me."

Exercise Two

The next step in changing your relationship blueprint is to create an intention statement that will replace your current blueprint with one that is more in tune with what you really want. Focus on any positive relationships in your life—that is, those relationships that have brought joy to you. If you are unable to do this, think of a healthy couple whom you admire. This could be a real couple or a television couple if necessary. Write a story about the positive relationship(s) as you think about them; be sure to include all of the things you admire about the relationship(s) in question. In this exercise, you can also list any positive traits that you experienced in previous relationships.

The next step may sound corny, but it is an important part of changing your blueprint and will help you to understand and comply with what you really want in a relationship.

- On a piece of paper (large enough to create a poster), draw or paste an image of "your man." Some people paste posters from magazines, while others draw their own (some even use stick figures).

- On that same piece of paper, use the positive attributes from the above exercise and list them as traits you want in a relationship. You may add to this list anything else that you feel you need in a relationship.

When you are done, you should have a poster with the man of your choosing surrounded by the positive attributes that you have come up with.

- Set an intention to attract the man you have drawn on your poster and say to yourself out loud, "I am entitled to joy in my life, and I call forth my proper soul mate and the pleasures of life that the Universe is waiting to release to me."

- Because we know there is no perfect individual, to keep it real and avoid setting yourself up for failure, you will need to list those traits that you don't like but can tolerate at the bottom of your poster. For instance, I don't like men who don't do laundry, but I will tolerate it.

- Share your list with a friend or therapist just in case you have normalized some abnormal behavior. Because of the nature of this step, working with a therapist is ideal.

When you are satisfied with your poster, you can make laminated copies of it and post it in areas of your house where you will be certain to see it (for example, the bathroom door or bedroom mirror).You can also make a wallet-sized copy to carry with you. Read it as often as you can, as doing so resets your blueprint. Over time, predators will no longer be attracted to you, and you will not be attracted to them.

Again, to enforce your new attitude, find a friend or preferably a therapist and share with that person your plan to enforce your new attitude. Share with this person any new relationships and ask them to hold you accountable should you attempt to slip back into old patterns.

CHAPTER SEVEN: WHILE YOU ARE WAITING

It will take time for your blueprint to reset. During this time, you will want to be very careful about developing any new relationships. You will also want to look at reinventing your life, minus predators, so that you are living and working toward your highest good in life. Finding a therapist or life coach can also help you deal with any residual anger and resentment related to the person or persons you released. I recommend looking for a therapist or life coach who practices mindfulness-based cognitive therapy and practices healing from within.

While you are focusing on your passion in life, you place yourself in a position to meet those who share your dreams. Before you meet your lifetime partner, you want to be in a place where you are doing those things that make you happy. By finding who you are and what makes you happy and by living out those values, you will make it easier for your rightful partner to recognize you.

Being in the waiting period does not mean that you can't date. However, it is important to keep in mind that until you are sure you are with your proper soul mate, you will want to guard your heart and your libido. You must do this if you want to avoid relationship drama. If you engage with a person who is not right for you, think of the possible consequences and ask yourself, is it worth it? Think of other things you could be doing, such as pursuing an education, your dream job, or a business venture you have always dreamed of.

Below are suggestions of things you may do while you are waiting.

Meditate on a Daily Basis

Meditation is a way to rid oneself of mind chatter. It is a way of practicing silence—a place where you learn to be with yourself without talking, without thinking, and without movement. It requires you to abstain from television, radio, phones, or other activities that distract from silence. Practicing silence will help you to clear mind chatter and pave the way for you to get in touch with what your body is saying to you. It is also a stress reliever and energy booster. One way of learning meditation is to purchase guided meditation CDs. There are also books on meditation that you can purchase or borrow from your local library. Best of all, see a therapist who practices meditation!

Affirm Yourself on a Daily Basis

Affirmations are a powerful way of resetting your blueprint for life and relationships. Develop the habit of affirming yourself every day using these powerful affirmations. You can also create your own affirmations.

- I am a dynamic expression of God.
- I am beautiful inside and out.
- I deserve genuine, unconditional love.
- I cherish and value who I am.
- I am number one in my life.
- I love me some (say your name).
- I intend to reach my highest good in life.
- I will allow my instincts to guide me.
- I am a powerful woman.
- I am brilliant.
- I take responsibility for my own life.
- I will live life to the fullest.

- I will surround myself with positive people.
- I will step out of my comfort zone and grow.
- I have the right to a life without predators.
- I will grow financially.
- I will love and take care of myself, knowing that only when I do so can I love and be there completely for others.

Be Your Own Best Friend and Lover

Learn to have a relationship with yourself, including taking yourself out. Learn to enjoy just being with yourself. Learn to do those little things that you would do for a lover for yourself. Aren't you worthy of those things too? Being clingy with another person and expecting him to make you happy is not an attractive trait and is a sign that you may be insecure. Research suggests that confidence is attractive; therefore, you need to be responsible for your own happiness, and you can only do so by learning to be your own best friend and enjoying being with yourself. This will boost your self-confidence. Enjoy a walk around the lake or take up golf lessons. You will be surprised at yourself and at who you might meet.

It Is Never Too Late to Return to School

If you have not finished high school or always wanted to go to college, now is the time to do so. It is never too late to educate yourself. Speak to a school counselor who can help you find your passion and go for it. There is financial aid available, and you may be lucky enough to get a scholarship. Get started now, and in two to four years, you can earn a degree and be on your way to finding your dream job. This could also mean more money for you to love yourself and take the dream vacation you have always wanted.

Financial Planning for the Future

Learn to create wealth in your life. It takes lots of energy to maintain a lifestyle of broke and poor; therefore, if you have trouble with finances, now is the time to learn to play the money game and use your energy to create wealth for yourself. If you are broke, tell yourself that being broke and poor is not an option and commit to striking a balance financially. Find a financial advisor and learn to invest and save, even if you only save a dollar a week. You want to develop the habit of saving and investing now, so when you have more, you will save and invest more. If you are well off financially, take the time to protect your assets and secure your financial future. Be a mentor for someone who needs help with finances.

Take Care of Your Health

Keep in mind that if you are not caring for yourself, you will not be able to care for anyone else. As stated earlier, a woman who is breastfeeding a baby has to feed herself before she can produce milk for her baby. If she fails to do so, neither she nor her child will survive. If you have children, they depend on you to be there for them. Taking care of your health will enable you to be there when your children graduate, get married, and have children of their own. Lastly, you need your health and strength to embrace your proper soul mate when he shows up. Take care of your health!

Overcome Your Fears and Focus on the Outcome You Want

Although some fears may be natural, fear in general can be immobilizing. It is natural to fear walking in front of a car or walking down a dark alley at night in a crime-ridden neighborhood. However, fear in general is responsible for many failures in life. Instead of allowing fear to control you, focus on the outcomes you want. Your thoughts, whether positive or negative, will actually lead to some action related to your thoughts. If you are focused on negative thoughts, you may very well fulfill your prophecy. If you want positive outcomes, your thoughts need to be positive. Having positive thoughts will lead you to take action steps that will lead to the outcome you really want. This is why positive affirmations are so powerful.

Form Relationships with Women Who Are Positive and Supportive

You will need to surround yourself with women who are positive and who support your growth. Take note of how you feel with the women you choose to support you and whether these relationships enhance your life. You only have so much time in one day, and you cannot afford to spend any of it combating negativity. How a person makes you feel usually tells you a lot about how that person feels. Therefore, if you are around people who feel good, they will radiate positive, supportive energy. If they don't feel good, it will be the opposite. Negative energy is toxic and hard to combat, which means it is in your best interest to avoid those who radiate negative energy.

You also want to be around women who support your growth by their actions. There is a difference between someone who supports you and someone who just makes comforting statements to you. If someone makes comforting statements to you but withholds information that can support your growth, it becomes questionable as to whether that person is actually supportive of you. Surround yourself with women whose actions suggest that they want to see you grow and are willing to lead you to the resources that will help you to grow.

Nurture Your Spirituality

Every one of us is in a different place spiritually, and no matter where you fit in this realm of things, know that there is a power greater than yourself. The Universe has a divine and unique order to it. It is our responsibility to find our connectedness to the Universe and seek our divine purpose on this planet and fulfill it.

Peace and blessings to you!

CHAPTER EIGHT: CASE SCENARIO

The following is a case scenario based on a real-life story. After reading this story, take some time to reflect on what you have learned from this book and then write down your thoughts. Think about how this scenario may reflect what's going on in your life or the life of someone you know. Discuss whether you believe that Glenda's instincts were dull or damaged. How was Gary able to pick up on her vulnerabilities? How was Gary able to keep Glenda emotionally stuck? You may want to make a list of other questions that would be important for you to discuss with your friends or therapist. You can also make this a book discussion with a group of supportive friends or with others who are struggling with predatory relationships. Make sure your discussion includes what you think needs to happen for Glenda, based on what you have learned from this book, so that she can move on.

Case Scenario

Glenda is a forty-six-year-old, recently widowed female. She had been married for twenty-three years. Her husband was diagnosed with cancer and died ten months later. Six months later, Glenda, feeling sorry for herself and lonely for attention and affection, joins her girlfriends for a night out at a club where she meets Gary.

Ordinarily, Glenda does not go to clubs, but she was convinced by well-wishers to go out and enjoy life for a change. Gary is spotted standing up against the wall staring directly at Glenda. Her friends point out to her that she has an admirer, and Gary later goes to the bar and sends Glenda a drink. After she accepts the drink, he comes over and joins Glenda and her friends. He charms her away from her friends, and they go off to another area of the bar where he dances with her and shows her a good time. He even buys her a flower before she joins her friends to leave for the night.

Glenda tells her friends what a good time she had with Gary; he held her close as they danced and made her feel special. She thinks that God has sent her an angel to heal her lonely heart and make her feel whole again. One of her friends sees right through Gary and warns Glenda to be careful, but she dismisses her friend as being jealous.

For the next three weeks, Glenda and Gary spend a lot of time on the phone talking; he tells her stories and makes her laugh. He tells her the tender woman story, and she tells her friends what a wonderful storyteller he is. He tells jokes and keeps her rolling in laughter. He tells her to be careful with her heart and then adds, "Don't get hooked." At the same time, Gary asks Glenda if she could ever love again and tells her he needs her to give him her heart if they are going to be in a relationship. Gary promises Glenda that he will take care of her sexually and emotionally and begins to use sexually explicit language as a matter of foreplay. She starts to dream about having the fairy tale romance with hot and steamy sex.

Gary sweeps Glenda off her feet with roses on Valentine Day and an Easter basket on Easter morning. Glenda, convinced that he really cares about her, decides to give in to him sexually, and he pleasures her beyond her wildest dreams. Gary asks for her heart during the act of sex, and she yields to him completely. He has captivated her heart and libido, and she is totally unaware of his motives. Soon after their first sexual encounter, he moves in with her, and the games begin.

Gary strings Glenda along sexually, getting her excited with sex talk but not following through. One day he asks for money for a down payment on a car so he can get a better job and take care of her. (Gary does not have a job but has led Glenda to believe he is working during the day while she herself is at work.) When Glenda hesitates, Gary questions whether she really cares about him and their relationship. He makes her feel guilty and threatens to get another woman to help him, because she does not care about him. Afraid that she may lose him, Glenda gives in. Immediately after she gives him a check, he gives in to her sexual needs. She is totally unaware of the set up and feels relieved after he delivers sexually. At that point, Glenda believes even more that he cares for her.

A few weeks after Gary gets his new car, he begins to banter with Glenda over little things and starts to accuse her of cheating. He demands that she call him to check in throughout the day and let him know her whereabouts. If she does not answer her phone at work, he questions what she was doing. Gary then starts to come home late and blames Glenda, stating that he is tired of arguing. The reality is that he is supposed to be working and looking for a better job; however, he is spending time with his next victim.

Gary starts to accuse Glenda of not caring about him and denies her sex. He tells her that he is stressed over the frequent arguing and that he cannot pay his car note. He demands that she pay it, because she is the reason he can't seem to find a better job so he can pay it himself. He promises her things will get better if she were there for him when he needs her. She gives in and agrees to pay his car note until he can get a decent job. Glenda is totally unaware that he does not even have a job and that he has been spending time with other women during the daytime when he is supposed to be at work. He yields to her sexually after she agrees to pay his car note.

Gary continues to argue with her with the intent of breaking her spirit so he can be in total control. He only gives in to her sexually when she gives in to him financially. After months of highs and lows, Glenda starts to question his job search. Gary accuses Glenda of not loving or trusting him and threatens to leave her for another woman. He is now staying out all night, and she does not question him when he says he is working, although there is no financial evidence of this.

Gary denies Glenda sex unless she gives him money, and she is starting to feel insecure. She is afraid to question him and starting to feel suspicious of his whereabouts. She starts to question herself and whether she has demonstrated to him that she really cares about and loves him and starts to blame herself for what is going wrong in this relationship. Afraid that he may be with another woman, Glenda agrees to pay his car note and gives him money on a regular basis to make him happy. He gives her sex in exchange for money, and while she does not feel right about this, she convinces herself that things will be all right. She has successfully normalized the abnormal, and the predator, knowing that he is in full control, begins to further take advantage of her weakness.

Gary convinces Glenda to take out a second mortgage on her house and pay off his car so that the money can be used to pay for their wedding, although he has not asked her to marry him. Glenda, excited over what appears to be a marriage proposal, gives in and takes out a second mortgage on her house and pays off the car for Gary. Several weeks later, Gary's best friend comes over to warn Glenda that Gary is cheating on her and using her. Just as Gary walks in the door, the friend starts to fondle Glenda. Gary witnesses this and becomes enraged, calling Glenda all kinds of names and accusing her of cheating with his best friend. Gary walks out and does not give her a chance to explain what happened. He comes back later, removes his belongings, and tells Glenda he wants nothing more to do with her. Glenda tries unsuccessfully to explain what happened. She is now distraught and expresses to her friends that she is having thoughts of suicide. They try to help her to realize that Gary is a predator. They had tried to be there for her, but she was not able to hear them.

Later Glenda learns that Gary was spending time with another woman when he was supposed to be working. She spots the car that she paid for at the building where the other woman lives. She is hurt and confused and spends months trying to get him back, despite what happened.

Glenda feels empty and believes there is unfinished business with Gary, which makes it very difficult for her to move on. She is unable to detach, and logic and reasoning do not help or heal. She is unable to get into another relationship, because she is desperate for Gary to come back and make things right. Glenda spends months in therapy trying to heal from a broken heart. She eventually relocates to another city to get over this relationship and start life over.

SUGGESTED READING

I recommend the following books for your personal growth:

Kathryn Alice – *Love Will Find You*

Melody Beattie – *The Language of Letting Go*

Martha Beck – *Finding Your Own North Star*

Sandra Brown – *How to Spot a Dangerous Man*

Deepak Chopra – *The Seven Spiritual Laws of Success*

Deepak Chopra – *Spiritual Solutions*

Lisa Engelhardt and Karen Katafiasz – *Anger Therapy*

Robert Hare – *Without Conscience*

Jean Houston – *A Passion for the Possible*

Richard J. Leider – *The Power of Purpose*

Phil McGraw – *The Self Matters Companion: Helping You Create Your Life from Inside Out*

Caroline Myss – *Invisible Acts of Power: Personal Choices That Create Miracles*

Clarissa Pinkola Estes – *Women Who Run with the Wolves*

Eckhart Tolle – *A New Earth*

Eckhart Tolle – *The Power of Now*

Iyanla VanZant – *Living Through the Meantime: Learning to Break the Patterns of the Past and Begin the Healing Process*

Paramahansa Yogananda – *Inner Peace*

BIBLIOGRAPHY

Akradi, Bahrim. *Wise Beyond Our Years.* Experience Magazine, 2010.

Alice, Katherine. *Releasing a Person.* Canada: The Alice Tompkins Company, 2006.

Beck, Martha. *Finding Your Own North Star.* New York, New York: Three Rivers Press 2001.

Chopra, Deepak. *The Seven Spiritual Laws of Success.* San Rafael, California: Amber-Allen Publishing, 1993.

Hamilton, W. Sir. n.p., 1913.

Hare, Robert D. *Without Conscience.* New York, New York: The Guilford Press, 1999.

Pinkola-Estes, C. *Women Who Run With the Wolves.* New York, New York: Random House Publishing, 1992.

Tolle, Eckhart. *The Power of Now: A Guide to Spiritual Enlightenment*. Vancouver: Namaste Publishing, 1997.

UNFPA, *The State Of World Population: Ending Violence Against Women And Girls* 2000

CONTACT INFORMATION:

If you are in a dangerous situation and need help immediately please call 911 or the National Abuse Hotline at 1-800-799-SAFE (7233) or TTY 1-800-787-3224.

For information on upcoming teleseminars, booking a speaking engagement with Miranda Houston or information on, The Annual Women's Survivor Conference please visit our website at: TheWomensRetreatCenter.com or you may also send an email to **thewomensretreatcenter@comcast.net**.

For more information on services offered by The Wordsmith, contact: **francdj16@gmail.com**